Simple Machine Science

Wheels and Axles

By Daisy Allyn

Gareth Stevens
Publishing

Please visit our website, www.garethstevens.com. For a free color catalog of all our high-quality books, call toll free 1-800-542-2595 or fax 1-877-542-2596.

Library of Congress Cataloging-in-Publication Data

Allyn, Daisy
　　　　Wheels and axles / by Daisy Allyn.
　　p.　cm. – (Simple machine science)
Includes bibliographical references and index.
Contents: Bikes, cars, and more!—Moving forward—Fun with wheels—Easy to turn—What is a pulley?—What are gears?—Singapore flyer.
ISBN 978-1-4339-8156-2 (hardcover)
ISBN 978-1-4339-8157-9 (paperback)
ISBN 978-1-4339-8158-6 (6-pack)
1. Wheels—Juvenile literature　　2. Axles—Juvenile literature　　[1. Wheels
2. Axles　　3. Simple machines]　I. Title　II. Series
　　　　　　　　　　　2013
　　　　621.8—dc23

Published in 2013 by
Gareth Stevens Publishing
111 East 14th Street, Suite 349
New York, NY 10003

Copyright © 2013 Gareth Stevens Publishing

Designer: Katelyn E. Reynolds
Editor: Greg Roza

Photo credits: Cover, p. 1 Hemera/Thinkstock.com; pp. 3–24 (background graphics) mike.irwin/Shutterstock.com; pp. 5, 7, 9, 11, 17, 19, 21 iStockphoto/Thinkstock.com; p. 13 Svetlana Tikhonova/Shutterstock.com; p. 15 photosync/Shutterstock.com.

Printed in the United States of America

CPSIA compliance information: Batch #CW13GS: For further information contact Gareth Stevens, New York, New York at 1-800-542-2595.

Contents

Boldface words appear in the glossary.

Bikes, Cars, and More!

Wheels are simple machines that turn to do work. Wheels spin around a rod called an axle. Your bike has two wheels, and each turns around an axle. Cars have four wheels and two axles. What else uses wheels and axles?

wheel

axle

5

Moving Forward

Wheels and axles change spinning **motion** into forward motion. The bigger a wheel is, the farther it can go in a single turn. Some trucks have very big wheels. This makes it easier to move heavy loads.

7

Fun with Wheels

Wheels and axles make traveling easier and more fun! Bikes aren't the only things that use wheels to get around. A skateboard has two axles, and each axle has two wheels. Roller skates have four wheels, too.

Wheels at Work

Wheels and axles make moving things easier. Instead of pushing a heavy box along the ground, you can use a wagon to move it. Instead of carrying heavy bricks, you can move them in a **wheelbarrow**.

Easy to Turn

Some wheels and axles make it easier to turn things. The bigger the wheel, the easier it is to turn the axle. However, bigger wheels have farther to go to get work done. Some wheels have handles that make them easier to turn.

handle

13

A doorknob is a wheel. It's fixed to an axle that opens the door when it turns. It would be hard to open a door if you had to turn just the axle. The knob gives you something to grab and turn.

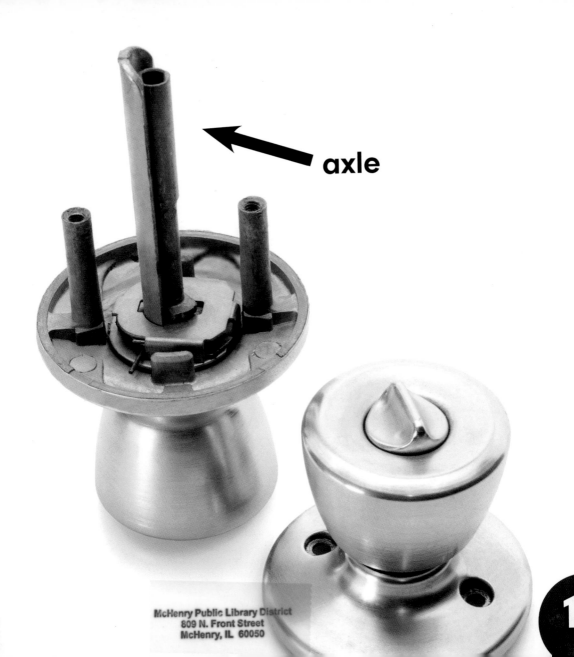

axle

What Is a Pulley?

A pulley is a simple machine that uses a wheel and axle. The wheel has a **groove** around the outer edge. This groove can hold a rope. When you pull down on one end of the rope, the other end goes up.

What Are Gears?

Many machines use special wheels called gears. Gears have teeth that fit together. When one gear turns, it turns other gears. The gears all stay put because they're on axles. Many clocks use gears. So do cars.

19

Singapore Flyer

The biggest wheel and axle in the world is a Ferris wheel. The Singapore Flyer has a **diameter** of 492 feet (150 m)! It takes about 30 minutes for the wheel to go all the way around once.

How We Use Wheels

bikes

cars and trucks

wagons

skateboards

roller skates

doorknobs

pulleys

wheelbarrows

gears

Glossary

diameter: the length of a line that passes from one side of a circle, through the center, and to the other side

groove: a narrow space cut into something

motion: movement

wheelbarrow: a tool that has a wheel, handles, and a place to hold and move things

For More Information

Books

Challen, Paul C. *Get to Know Wheels and Axles.* New York, NY: Crabtree Publishing, 2009.

Smith, Siân. *Wheels and Axles.* Chicago, IL: Heinemann Library, 2013.

Websites

Simple Machines
www.edheads.org/activities/simple-machines/
Learn about simple machines through this fun, interactive website.

Simple Machines Game
www.msichicago.org/fileadmin/Activities/Games/simple_machines/
Learn more about simple machines by playing a fun online game.

Singapore Flyer
www.singaporeflyer.com
Read more facts about the Singapore Flyer and see pictures of it.

Index